Alzheimer's
By
Barbara O'Donnell
ISBN: 978-1-8380464-3-9

Copyright 2020 Barbara O'Donnell

All rights reserved. No part of this publication may be reproduced, stored in a retrieval system or transmitted in any form or by any means, electronic, mechanical, photocopy, recording or otherwise, without prior written consent of the copyright owner. Nor can it be circulated in any form of binding or cover other than that in which it is published and without similar condition including this condition being imposed on a subsequent purchaser.

The right of Barbara O'Donnell to be identified as the author of this work has been asserted in accordance with the Copyright Designs and Patents Act 1988.

A copy of this book is deposited with the British Library

Published By: -

i2i
PUBLISHING

i2i Publishing. Manchester.
www.i2ipublishing.co.uk

ALZHEIMER'S!

'Where are they gone, the old familiar faces....

How some have died, and some have left me,
And some are taken from me; all are departed;
All, all are gone, the old familiar faces.'

(Extract from The Old Familiar Faces - Charles Lamb 1775-1834)

This book is dedicated to my mother, Bertha Wilkinson (nee Wilcock, 16.10.1921 – 12.03.2008).

She had been gradually getting more and more confused for about ten years before she died – and naturally, her mental state became worse over time. It also became unsafe for her to live alone. I looked after her twenty-four hours a day for the last four years of her life. To do this, I had the help of two trained nurses. Without their help I would have really struggled or found it an impossibility. I had my own business, I was studying: first with work-based qualifications, then I did a degree, then a PGCE and finally a Master's Degree. I also had four 'grown-up' children, one of whom was profoundly disabled. It wasn't easy!

Still, the decision was made. I rented out my own house, sold her bungalow – I had Enduring Power of Attorney – and moved us all into a house with a 'granny' flat that I'd seen for sale, using a mixture of her bungalow money and my own money. I rearranged the annexe to look like her bungalow so she would think in her confused state that she was going home after one of her stays in hospital. Her stays in hospital became quite frequent. From the late 90's onwards she'd had a series of falls; broken knees, bruises, blackouts – and every time she'd been checked out at hospital. As her lack of balance increased so did her loss of memory.

Naturally, like anyone with any pride, she was in total denial of this. And she was a damned good mimic of 'normal'. Everyone else had always 'got it wrong' – there was, "nothing wrong with my memory."
It was clear by 2004 that she had full-blown dementia and, after trying various 'care' agencies in her own home, it was also clear that the only person I could trust to do the job properly was me. Anything else – bar a care home (and even then…) – would have been unsafe. But first, a little about mum, who I often refer to as Bertha as it's such a comical name…

She was born in Preston, Lancashire and, for her, this was hallowed ground because her immediate family all lived there. Bertha had an overprotected adolescence. She had four older brothers and a very strict mother – my Nana – who believed that moral boundaries were there for a reason and that was the end of the subject. My Granddad, on the other hand, was very easy going but would vacate the house if it became too full and retire to his pigeon cote for a quiet life.

Bertha had an almost aristocratic sense that her family was the best; they could do no wrong (in-laws could, but not blood relations). She was a respectable, working-class snob. By contrast, my dad's family were 'rough', swearing, smoking, alcohol drinking, Geordie miners and she never let him forget this. Everything she possessed was, in her eyes, a potential heirloom - which she would give to you with the stock phrase, "look after it, it's a good one": even if it was a plastic popper necklace; that actually happened.

She had a great sense of humour and was very kind – to her family. She was generous with money to both her children and her seven grandchildren and she would do anything to help them. She was also narrow-minded, provincial and afraid of standing out from the crowd. She was a typical product of the way girls were brought up before and during the Second World War: you were either a good time girl, (that is, a tart to be looked down upon) or you were a good girl who stayed at home and practiced at becoming a good wife. No World War Two GI's for Bertha!

Her judgemental nature was not really her fault and I, in turn, do not mean to judge her too harshly. But she could be very difficult to live with; very pedantic and inflexible – there again, fairly typical of her respectable working-class background and her inherited morals, which, of course, were set in granite rather than stone. It was unfortunate for her that she brought up daughters in the period of sexual freedom that hallmarked the 1960's! – her Victorian values were much derided by me and my sister and I suppose we gave her just as hard a time as she gave us.

I know that she bitterly regretted getting married and having children. Her ideal life would have been to stay at home in Preston, look after her mum and dad and never move out of the little, safe bubble that she had almost cerebrally created. She idealised her past and constantly told the same stories, with exactly the same script, time and again. It was possible to mime these stories because of their repetition, behind her back of course, as cruel teenagers do - and find the act hilarious. If you said something like, "Mum, you've already told me loads of times" she would reply without deviation, "Well, I'll tell you again," with a determined look on her face!

Unlike my generation and maybe, unlike some of her own generation, my mother did not value girlfriends as confidantes, or someone to have fun with. They were all potential threats, especially if they had fun-loving personalities, smoked, drank, were good-looking - or sexy. As I was growing up, she was almost worse than a man for being morally judgemental towards her own gender. This, of course, meant that she had no girlfriends. It also meant that family were all important to her and ultimately (physically) close family – that is, me – had no choice but to look after her. Either that or leave her at the mercy of the care system. This also meant that, apart from our day trips out or my visits to her before I looked after her full-time, that she became very lonely. This couldn't have been more ironic as she had yearned to be alone and free to do what she wanted for years – as she never tired of telling us.

Before she began to show signs of Alzheimer's disease, she would snigger – albeit secretly and behind her hand - at those that she was forced to share the same space with who had mental health problems. This from a woman who had a disabled grandson! For example, when she fell and broke her kneecap, she ended up in a recovery ward shared by all kinds of elderly women. Some, of course, had dementia. One lady would get dressed in smart clothes and wait patiently; sat on a chair by the side of the ward entrance. She was waiting for her mother to pick her up then they could get the bus home. Bertha thought this was funny! This particular occasion was when she came out with the gem: "If I ever get like that shoot me!" Be careful what you wish for......

With every fall that she had, her descent into Alzheimer's accelerated. I began to realize that National Health nurses and doctors have no training in mental health issues – except for specific wards, like the psychiatric or geriatric wards – and consequently, she was treated like a naughty child by nurses young enough to be her grandchildren. I realised, by witnessing incidents, the utter humiliation of the elderly people at the hands of callous nurses who behaved like they themselves were on stage with the patients as their captive audience. It was expected that the patients were to laugh along with them. This was the only social interaction that they got – apart from visiting times.

The elderly who could not feed themselves were ignored or worse told: "Are you not eating that then?" The food or drink was then whisked away from them with an accompanying patronising shake of the head and roll of the eye. Deliberate cruelty was endemic. Old ladies and men were left asking politely for a bed pan to no avail. They were completely ignored - then 'told off' if they could no longer control their bowels or bladder – therefore messing the bed. There were some excellent nurses, but they were far outnumbered by the appalling ones.

My only solution as she descended towards oblivion was to care for her myself – my sister lived in Wales and I was the local one. I'd already cared for her in her own home but the move to the house with the granny annexe was a very long and utterly exhausting four years....

You Don't Have to Be Rich

She lived in Ashmoor Street
A basic 2 up 2 down
With outside toilet
In Preston.

She was the last of 5
All of them boys
The only girl
In the world.

You don't have to be rich
To be spoiled
By your family
And friends...

She was brought up to be seen
And not heard
By anyone
At all.

She was meant to smile
And be quiet
And good - like
A girl.

You don't have to be rich
To be spoiled
By your family
And friends...

Men were a threat to her
Though she flirted
And giggled
With them

Liking the attention, coyly smiling
Being found attractive
But no more
Than that

You don't have to be rich
To be spoiled
By your family
And friends...

A Brief Precis of Her/Our Life

Part 1

She was always right – she said so!
She was never wrong – she couldn't be!
She was a perfect person – but perfection doesn't exist
As she no longer does.

She loved to cuddle - babies and toddlers.
Uncomfortable with adults contact; very shy.
'Good girls are quiet and they smile,' Nana boomed.
That stayed with her.

She was always right – raised to be 'good'
Her brothers went dancing – she could not
Her friends dated American GI's – she did not.
She was perfect, you see.

She married - waiting - just after the War
She and dad lived with her parents in Preston.
For five years! She wanted to stay with her mum and dad
(Not perfect for him).

Part 2

She was always right – she was alone
In Blackpool; with two children - dad worked,
Then: the pub. Too critical to make friends of women -
They'd have to be perfect.

A toddler - I would be a seagull
From the built-in seats on Blackpool prom
I would fly into her arms - She always caught me!
She was perfect then.

She was always right – I was five
Sexually assaulted by a boy aged 9:
She screamed and cried and really scared me -
I was no longer perfect.

We'd watch the Miss World Contest on TV
'There's better looking girls on the street!'
She'd say. Yet she never, ever complimented them –
(Or me for that matter).

Part 3

She was always right – I passed my 11+
And entrance exam! But I was never good enough
For her exacting standards. I knew she loved me - but
I just wasn't perfect.

A teenager - I wanted a new frock.
'Sit on your dad's knee and give him a cuddle!
You'll get it.' - Strange advice from a perfect person?
Freudian slip showing!

She was always right – 'You don't play fair
With men!' She'd gasp - outraged at Joan's naivety.
Fluttery and flirty with men herself - but slightly scared...
Definitely not perfect!

She reminisced about her past - *constantly*
Longing for its return - before adulthood and marriage,
Before sex, before responsibility, before monotony, before
Time changed everything.

Part 4

She was always right – 'She should have married
A bloody vicar!' Dad would say mantra-like.
Wrong!
She should never have married at all – but stayed in
Preston.
In her own past.

But not just Preston! – She longed for those people
Who populated the stories of her 'perfect'
childhood.
Re-told again and again: in the rosy landscape of
Bertha's mind
And wishful thought.

She was always right – 'It always happens to
Barbara!'
She'd sadly drone. I was the intended victim. For a
while
It worked: a teenage inferiority! She wanted
perfection -
A mini-Bertha!

She 'found' my pill – in my handbag.
Shock! Horror! Hysterics! - I was a 'tart':
Did she really want me to have a shot-gun
wedding?
(I had one anyway).

Part 5

She was always right – 'You think you're perfect
Don't you?' I'd say. 'Well… I am!' she'd counter.
Smug and serious! Eye-rolling dad wanted a quiet life.
So he just agreed.

'If you had your time again – what would you do?'
She thought: then … 'I'd stay at home, never marry,
Nor have children - no offence.' - 'None taken!' I said!
'No shit', I thought.

She was always right - 'You'll miss me when I'm gone!'
I laughed it off as doom-ridden, old lady talk.
Her fear of death kept her alive longer than she should -
But this one time she was spot on.

She was always right – she said so!
She was never wrong – she couldn't be!
She was a perfect person – and perfection doesn't exist
As she no longer does.

Berth's Way of 'Mingling' Walking

She would walk everywhere.
She really enjoyed it!
An exercise that she could bear
Her way of keeping fit.

Just one of many ways
Of staving off her loneliness
She could meet people, and say
A greeting: without fear of oddness.

She saw them, yet did not engage
With them... except for the greeting.
Ideal for her! No need for rage
No need for emotional meeting!

This did not do her any good,
Long-term. No actual connection.
She could observe, she judged – she could!
Not inter-action, more di-section.

**First Signs
Descent**

Enter Bertha...
'How's your mother?'
She'd ask Eamon.
'She's fine, Bertha'
He'd answer'
Smiling.

Seconds later…
'How's your mother?'
She'd ask again.
He'd look at me
Half-laughing -
Incredulous.

I'd say to her...
'You've just said that!'
'Well I'll say it again!'
She'd say.
On purpose?
Just to annoy?

Entirely possible...
Being Bertha.
On the wind-up,
Irritating.

But not this time...
Oh no.

And not ever after.

**To the Virgins, (Bertha) to Make Much of Time
(With apologies to Robert Herrick, 1591-1674)**

Gather ye faculties while ye may,
Old time is still a-flying
And this same Bertha that smiles today,
Tomorrow will be dying

The glorious girl of earth was fun,
But fainter she's a-getting,
The sooner will her race be run
And nearer she's to setting.

That age was best (which was her first),
When youth and blood were warmer -
Alive in Preston! The worse and worst
Of times succeed the former.

Then be not shy but use your time
And maybe even marry;
For having lost but once your prime,
You WILL forever tarry.

The Non-Driver
Driving Miss Bertha

Its ritual – every Wednesday and Sunday
I drive Miss Bertha.
Just familiar routes to jog her fading memory:
Preston, down the promenade, around town.

This time - 'I need the toilet!' Desperate!
We've just left Preston
On a no-stopping road with greenery everywhere
Then it comes to me – Warton: McDonald's!

Foot down – time of the essence
Going way too fast!
An awful smell begins to permeate the car
'Nearly there!' I encourage; desperate…

Screech to a halt in the Drive Thru car park
Got to get to the loos!
The smell does not improve as I help Bertha to the Ladies
'Hang on, nearly there!' I plead.

Get her into the pristine toilet! – It is
Indeed too late.
I clean her with the help of paper towels and liquid soap

A bag of some kind for her underwear?...

Get Bertha into the car and belt her in
(With a seat-belt!).
Go the counter for a random bag to hide her shame
They give me one for a Happy Meal!

Off we go again - back in the car
I drive Miss Bertha
She glares at me, 'We didn't even have a coffee!'
And, 'What's that smell – is it the dog?'

Raging Incontinence
Smell

Her house is now starting
To smell *really* bad.
It's not just her wind,
Just that would be sad

Enough! No, it's incontinence
That she's not addressing.
I've tried to talk sense
To her – she carries on messing.

How to approach her
When she's in denial -
Without my upsetting her?
Now that's the real trial.

She shuffles from room
To room, trailing with pee.
Her carpets will soon
Rot - and then what will be?

'Can you smell something mum?'
I broach, tentatively.
'What like?' she returns, with some
Passion: de-fensively.

'Like pee' I say clearly.
Have you wet yourself?'
'Of course I've not – nearly! -
But just stopped myself.'

She's on Fantasy Island
She's sat - soaking wet -
But would rather pretend
She's OK...and I'd like to bet

That she'll never own up to her incontinence.
So I clean up the pee.
And I pay the full penance
For living nearby her - and just being me.

Aedh Wishes for the Cloths of Heaven (With apologies to W.B. Yeats, 1865-1939)

Had I but thought that this would come,
En-wrought with such a lot of shite,
This state of mind to which she's come
Of night and light and so much shite,
I wish that she didn't get under my feet;
But I, being alone, have only my dreams
And nightmares. What will be under my feet?
Her of course! – and she treads on my dreams.

The Surprise Party
Eightieth Birthday – 2001

I'd planned it all – with a little help from the kids.
Joan couldn't come – there were serious health reasons.
Bertha was entirely in the dark!

Two living friends, three of my kids and two of Joan's boys,
Great-grand children! I was quite excited, pulling it together
Then I got the phone call.

'Where are you? I've been waiting for half an hour!'
It was the day of her birthday, but she was set in her routine
Of 11am - not 6pm, as arranged.

She was convinced that I was taking her
To the shops – I was in the wrong, naturally; (she was always right).
I almost called the whole thing off.

But I didn't. I gritted my teeth and admitted
MY mistake. Then I put down the phone and eye-rolled at a
Sniggering Caz…..'For fuck's sake!'

Half-past five! I gather the kids (adults, really)
Into the car. The cake! I send the boys – Bobby and Tommy -
To *carefully* get it from the house.

The cake is placed in the road. I open the boot...
Everyone argues! We set off! I have to get the cake and the kids
There on time... break-neck speed!

We get to the restaurant at 5.40pm.
Good going! The kids jump out of the car. 'Where's the cake?'...
It's in the road - outside my house!

I screech back to the house. It's still there!
And it's in one piece! Unbelievable! No time to drop the cake off ...
Must pick-up Bertha on time.

I'm outside her bungalow. No sign of life...
I look in through the window and she's in her armchair, asleep
With gaping mouth – an effigy of death.

I bang on the window – she wakes!
Surprised to see me! 'What have you come at this time for?' I swallow

A strong urge to say, 'Why the fuck do you think?'

I persuade her that we've arranged this,
And that we must get a move on! She slowly goes to the loo,
She slowly combs her hair! …People are waiting!!

I get her in the car with the cake (hidden)
On the back seat. 'Where are we going?' I crush the desire
To say: 'To a fucking restaurant!' – instead…'Ah ha!'

We finally get there at 6.10pm – not bad considering.
We walk in and sat in the foyer are relatives and two live friends.
'Surprise!' says everyone, and then, 'Happy Birthday!'

She's pleased! Her eyes fill up – she smiles!
She very slowly recognises relatives. One-by-one, taking it all in.
I get the cake to one of the waiters. She scans the scene….

'Where's Joan?' she says. Everyone covers for her.
Bertha's got no time to be upset, she's surrounded by grandchildren

Great-grandchildren, and her two living mates.

She loved her night! There's photos of her laughing!
I had to stay sober because I was driving the OAP's home.
Couldn't wait to smoke Camel and drink Gin!

The Descent
The Fall

I got a call from Eamon.
At 4pm. It's Bertha.
She's had a fall – she's at the Vic
Her knee's gone black.

I'm in Preston with Caz!
In Debenhams.
We're clothes shopping!
I have to get back.

I go straight there.
She's in a bad way
A doctor is draining her knee
She's *smiling* at him.

'We have to keep her in'
He says. How long?
I say. 'Depends on her recovery',
Says the doctor...

The A & E ward is full of drunks
And smack-heads.
This is no place for Bertha, alone!
Smiling, Alzheimer's and old.

She finally gets a bed
A *mixed* ward!
This is wrong! She can't stay here
Alone! I'll have to stay with her.

The night is tempered by howls
And the screams of drunks and addicts
I try to doze but must keep alert -
For Bertha's sake.

The morning rounds between 7 and 9
She finally gets seen
But no one talks directly to her...
Even though she smiles (!)

And this happens again and again.....

Sudden Light – with apologies to Dante Gabriel Rossetti (1828-82)

I have been here before
Time upon time I cannot tell
I know that she's behind the door
The sour, rank smell,
The little sounds, the lights under the door.

You have been here before
Just now it's getting less and less
But just when I think there is no more
You tend to do your best.
Top at playing normal; the lights under the door.

Has this been thus before?
When did it start - and did you fight
With crosswords/word search - your brain to restore?
Deception! But despite
This cover of yours; it can't go on much more.

The Fallacy of Care
Care in the Community

I hire a care company to look after Bertha in her own home.
This may free me up!
I'll still look in of course, I'll be a good daughter, check she's OK!

Ideally - They come first thing in the morning to get her changed
Meals on wheels come at lunchtime.
Another carer comes about 6pm – pretty good, I think!

Reality - Bertha looks at the 'carers' through her porch window
She *smiles* back at them
She politely refuses to let them in and staggers back to her TV chair.

She's in her nighty and has soiled and wet herself
They believe in CHOICES.
They say 'OK Bertha - we'll call back tomorrow if you won't let us in'.

I am working full-time, doing a degree and completing my RMA

I call in to see if she's OK.
She is covered in stains at the front of her nighty
and shit at the back.

She hasn't eaten, she hasn't washed and she hasn't
got dressed
They believe in CHOICES.
Bertha has dementia - she can't even choose what
she wants to wear!

So much for my freedom! 'You can't trust anyone
these days'
Comes back to haunt me.
This clearly can't go on – something must be done;
by me of course...

I'll give them fucking CHOICES.

Leisure – or Care Work/Nursing (with apologies to W.H.Davies, 1871-1940)

What is this life if full of 'care'
We've lots of time to stand and stare! –

Time to stand around and talk
And stare - as long as it's called work?

Time to see, when beds we pass
Where we ignore pleas for a glass

Of water. And a bedpan too -
Let them sit in their own poo!

No time for work – that's not for me!
Just look busy, smile, you'll see!

No time for cleaning or feeding too
I do what I like - So go and sue!

A poor life this if old and ill
Best end it all and take that pill.

My Brilliant Idea
The Move

I know! The idea comes to me like a lightening flash...
I'll find a house with a granny flat!
I'll organise her care and keep an eye on her!
Brilliant idea.

After about three months of hard searching I find it...
The ideal house with a granny flat!
I'll get two trained nurses and me to look after her
Brilliant idea.

Bertha has another fall and whilst she's in the Vic...
I sell her bungalow immediately (it's 2005)!
Then I thought, 'I'll start work – I'll clear her garage'
Fucking nightmare.

Bertha has kept everything – even old newspapers...
I search them for any relevance!
Weddings, Christenings, GCSE or A level results,
Births or Deaths.

Nothing! They're just old magazines and newspapers...

Then there's all the other stuff!
Bertha's phrase, 'Don't throw it away – it's a good one'
Travels round my head.

Then there's in inside of the bungalow and her belongings...
An unbelievable amount of utter crap!
I ruthlessly keep only her familiar bits, furniture and clothes
Fucking nightmare.

I rearrange them in the granny flat, it looks great...
Exactly as they were in her bungalow!
I even get a safe, electric, living-flame fire for the lounge
Brilliant idea.

Now all I have to do is move in myself with all *my* stuff...
Then synchronize Bertha's move from the Vic!
Six weeks of their recommended (i.e. cheap) agency staff -
Brilliant idea.

Or fucking nightmare....?

For Bertha – With apologies to John Pudney (1909-77)

Do not despair
For Bertha, head-in-air
She will be as sound
As Bertha underground

Fetch out her pounds
(*Her* head's in the clouds)
And keep all your tears
For her in after years

Better for her
To have some paid care
And keep your own head
To see her safe, instead.

Trained Apes
The Staff

They come: one after the other
Each one as crap as the last
A man – looking like a Hairy Biker
Wanting to wash her down!
A tattooed lady – to 'give Bertha her medication'
(She doesn't take any).

Here, the non-English speaking staff
There, the untrained teenager
Followed by the moron
Who believes in **choices** etc., etc.
Meaning I had to change Bertha and constantly see
Her front bottom.

This carried on for about two months
Each one as crap as the last
In which time, through friends
And colleagues - I found Annabelle
And Maureen. Brilliant, proper, trained nurses
Thank Christ.

Annabelle and Maureen both have holidays
They have lives
And other jobs, naturally
Sometimes they can't make it

Meaning that the care falls to me, just me, only me
By myself.

Oh, some of her grandchildren help, of course.
They try hard when they can.
But it's me – pretending to be her mother
A neighbour; her best-mate; a stranger.
She's forgotten *she's* a mother. She's only a kid!
Oh bollocks...

Entertainment
The Television

I pop into the annexe to say
Goodnight to Bertha, as is my way.
She's got the television on
I'll do the usual, then begone!

She blankly stares at the TV screen
Whilst rocking to and fro. She's seen
A man she thinks she recognises
Who is he Mum? – There are no prizes

For the answer to this teaser.
I'll say some names, now that'll please her.
Is it Jack Hilton? An old mate -
No not him, this one's a state!

Is one of dad's friends on the tele?
Then she remarks, He's lost his belly!
He used to be a big fat thing
He needs some food, he's thin as string!

She reaches for her Kipling cake
And leans towards the 'man' to make
Him eat a bit, to put on weight -
(And all she's got's this bit of cake!)

She shoves French Fancy at the 'man'
Then leans back, pleased, so that she can
Say that she helped him have some grub...
The cake slides down the screen then, thud!

It falls upon the non-slip floor. (It would).
She looks appalled; of course, (she should!)
Someone has made a mess with cake!
In her front room! The rat! The snake!

She looks around – accusing me.
'Cos it's just me and her, you see.
No one else could have made this mess…
It must be Barbara – lucky guess!!

Starry, Starry Night
My Night Off

One Sunday night, Eamon and I
Manage to go and have a curry.
I have to put her to bed – no cover.
No probs! I've had a little break
And a good night, and a little drink.

I enter through her front door
And she's smiling, looking alert
And interested! Now that's a turn up!
I'm still in a frock, on going out mode,
And perfumed, and a little pissed.

She looks at me and I recognise -
The Look! She thinks I'm young tonight!
'Did you have a good time?' – she says,
 Beaming. 'I did mum – a right laugh!'
'And did your lot meet anyone?'

I play along. 'Oh yes! We met these lads!'
I say. 'Oh yes?' She countered.
 'I hope that you behaved yourself.'
'Course I did mum! We've danced
To Tamla Motown records all night!'

She really smiles. She's Sunday's Child -
Fair of face, full of grace, bonny, blithe
And good all day. Then...she's gone – to where?
'Can I go home now?' She says, frightened.
'Course you can, but have a little nap first.'

I persuade. She wants her mother,
She wants her dad, she wants her brothers -
All of them: dead. And now she's getting ready
To go. But when?? I wonder; as I change
Her adult nappy and apply her rash lotion.

Poor Bertha! She really would have hated
To be this figure of fun - (as she would see it).
Couldn't have lived with me seeing her naked,
Or confused, or double incontinent. Dispossessed,
Disorientated, unhappy and alone.

She wanders Lonely as a Cloud
With apologies to William Wordsworth (1770-1850)

She wanders lonely as a cloud
That floats on high o'er Preston town
When all at once she saw a shroud...
A host of long dead relatives;
Beside the shops, beneath the River
There they were – (suppress a shiver).

Continuous as her long lost mind
Forever wandering on its way,
They stretched in never-ending line
Along the Ribble, in the bay:
One Hundred saw she at a glance,
Waving and welcoming in gentle dance.

The water beside them danced; but they
Floated on air: all-smiling, free
Bertha could not be owt but gay
In such familiar company:
She gazed - and gazed – but did not think
That they were leading her to the brink:

For often when she's in her chair
In vacant or a confused mood
They come to her in her despair

(Which is the hell of solitude).
And then her heart fills up with pleasure,
Her golden past – that, she *does* treasure.

Human Detritus
Shit

It's everywhere.
The smell hits you.
Maureen has another job to go to,
So has Annabelle.
They only work
Four hours a day
They've got other jobs,
And they have holidays.
I don't.

Where to start?
Bertha can hardly walk.
She's covered in shit; and pee
It's everywhere.
I get her to the shower seat.
'Where's mother?'
She says, smiling.
'She said you could stay the night'
I say.

I remember...
Before Alzheimer's.
She was in hospital
After a fall.
And was openly laughing

At a patient with dementia
'Waiting for a bus'.
'If I get like that – shoot me!',
She said.

Where's that gun?...

The Bertha (With apologies to William Blake, 1757-1827)

Bertha, Bertha spewing shite
In the annexe, through the night
What would you think if you could see
Yourself - surrounded by your pee?

And in what distant memories
Are you living? Are you free?
What did you hope? What did you dream?
How did you get to be so mean?

And what *did* make you hate the tart
(So that you seemed to have no heart?)
Looked down your nose at all things bold...
(This judgement stopped as you got old).

What the nonsense, what the pain
In what confusion was your brain?
What the tablets, what the meds
If no one knows what's in your head?

When your mind started to go
And you were lost and did not show
To anyone your dread and fear
-No doubt, at first, a lonely tear.

Bertha, Bertha - you did alright!
Throughout the darkness of your night
You were safe and you were clean
It could have been a much worse scene!!

Real Descent
The First Stroke

Her face smiling at a crazy angle
Her arm bent behind her back
Her legs trapped under her body
I can't believe she's still alive

She's been there all night
By the cold feel of her. But
She doesn't know that she's cold
That she's old, or who I am

She may have broken something
Phone the doctor for a visit
Get her checked out...
You never know – she can't tell you

Quick visit from the doctor:
'Yes she can stay where she is
Have I got help?' 'Oh yes...
There's me Maureen and Annabelle'.

There's Meals on Wheels
Once - at dinner time only.
There's OAP Playschool
Ten 'till 3, Monday to Friday.

All to be paid for by her
None of it free to her
All of it endured by her
As she just wants to sit.

What else could I do?
I'm clinging on here
By the skin of my teeth
Whatever that means.

I promised her, you see.

'When I get old, don't put me into a Home'

Little Bertha Lost – with apologies to William Blake (1757-1827)

'Mother! Mother! Where are you going?
O do not leave me here.
Speak, mother speak to your little girl
Or I shall fill with fear.'

The night was dark, no mother was there;
Bertha was all alone.
The pavements were bleak and she did weep
Dementia – now she must atone.

**Depressing Journey
Pushing Miss Bertha**

It's all uphill
Quite literally

Blackpool promenade
May look flat

But believe me
It's not.

I'm pushing
Thirteen stone's worth

Of the muscle-less
Flabby body

Of Alzheimer's woman
Who has no sense

Of balance -
As well as no sense.

She keeps trying
To escape the chair

Which does not make

For an easy ride.

I buy us both
An ice-cream

I feed her fave
Her tutti-frutti

A wap bop a loo bop
Ba lap bam boom.

She enjoys
Her ice cream.

She stares
But can no longer see

She breathes
But is no longer alive

She smiles
But can no longer speak

Sometimes, this
Is a good thing

And other times
Like now -

When I would
Like to talk

To her
About old times

And funny things
That happened

And have
A real laugh

Whilst she's
Eating her tutti frutti

Enjoying herself...

It's shit.

Nearly the End
The Second Stroke

Bertha lying on the floor
In the annexe; by the door.
Is she living, is she dead?
It's hard to tell, she's by the bed.

Need some help to pull her out
Can't pull alone, I need some clout.
Maureen's due at 7 a.m.
I'll have to try alone till then.

Maureen's early, thank-you God!
She comes straight in and with a nod
We count to three and pull together
Up she comes, but it is whether

During the night she may have had
A stroke! Hard to tell, but it looks bad.
Her face is blank and it's pulled down
Her eyes stare though me, dark and brown.

We'll have to call the paramedics -
We'd rather not, 'cos some are real pricks –
We have no choice, we can't do this
Things have gone awry, amiss!

At the hospital, both admitted,
Maureen goes and Bertha's billeted
She doesn't know what's going on
Tries to dismount the trolley that she's put on.

Moves towards the end of it
Can't even walk! – Will drop like a brick!
I grip her on the trolley by force
Whilst nurses and young doctors course

By: but no one comes to us, not yet
(They will if she falls, I'd like to bet).
Then we're approached by a very young man,
I'm the speech therapist – I am!

'I come to assess your mother's speech'
'But she can't talk', I tell him (Shriekkkk)!
But: 'She needs to do this test for records
Then, we'll assess her for the wards.'

He doesn't seem to understand
That her brain has turned to sand.
(You stupid little PC goffer!
Where's commonsense?) So I then proffer...

'She cannot walk, she cannot talk
She's like a baby - (not age appropriate!)
She cannot understand one word

Of what you're saying' – (you little turd!)

'And please don't tell her to **behave**!'
Bertha, shuffling, needs to be saved
From falling meanwhile off the trolley.
'This is why I'm here!' (you Wally)

He doesn't get it – he isn't trained
In mental health, he answers, pained.
'I tell you what,' I say to Kildare,
'I'll take her home, she's better off there.'

Living Death
Transition

It all becomes too much for me
I'm losing weight, can't even see
An end to it – except her death.
She's alive but only draws her breath
As proof of living. No mind, just matter.
Too many strokes: and I'm shattered.

I always promised that I would
Look after her and never should
I put her into 'care'. She's not aware
That she's alive. - She's back there -
To that place where she was most happy,
At home when she was a little chappie.

I look around for suitable 'homes'
Where she would not be just a clone
Of an old person, and that she would
Be properly cared for, as she should
Be - but... how to find the perfect place?
They may just look good to your face.

Fortunately 'care' is my area
Of expertise. I can be warier
Than most – because I know how bad
Some are. 'God's waiting rooms' and very sad.

I'll start to check them out and visit them.
And seek advice from those who know them.

Her GP recommends some names to me
And I visit them quite feverishly
I need to find a place - and quick!
Bertha's really very sick
She's an empty vessel waiting to die
I did my best – but why oh why

Did she have to go this way? – it's shit
(Quite literally). At least I think I've done my bit.
These years have been completely heartbreaking
I've become a madwoman in the making
At least she's not aware at all
That she has gone right up the wall.

She cannot walk, she cannot talk, no sounds
Can pass her lips at all. She needs to be bound
By straps to keep her in her chair
She's even losing most of her hair.
Her teeth went one-by-one just lately
She's curled up now but stood so stately

When she was younger. She never slouched
That wasn't her – it would make the body pouched.
Walked everywhere and tried to keep fit
Her constant falls are what did it.

They changed her – lost her confidence
Making her housebound and losing her senses.

I've found the ideal home for her – Hurrah!
It's called Bank House and is near the River Wyre
Had she been sane she would have loathed it
Alzheimer's though – she won't give a shit!
It's clean and does not stink of pee
Which they all have seemed to do, to me.

It's countrified – that's why she'd hate it
But the staff are top - and are paid to clean shit.
I know I can trust them. And, because Bertha is quiet,
She's put with the 'normals' and won't cause a riot.
They seem happy to be there – that's good!
My conscience is eased a bit: I hoped that it would.

Parting - With Apologies to Emily Dickinson (1830-86)

Her life closed twice before its close;
Yet she remains to see
If her belief of nothingness
Will be the truth for she,

So grim, the outlook for her now
Two strokes that did befell
Parting is all we know of Heaven,
And all we need of hell.

Death
The End – 12th March 2008

Apparently my phone rang
At 6am, but I didn't hear it.
It rang again at 7am
This time I was up
And got the phone.

It was Joan! 'There's no easy
Way to say this Barb' she said.
'Bank House phoned me
This morning at 6am
To tell me Bertha died.

They found her on the rounds
In the morning – she must
Have died peacefully
In her sleep.'
I put down the phone.

Why did Joan
Have to find out first?
I was the one doing all
The graft. Of all days
To oversleep!

I told Eamon, then said:

'I'm an orphan! Enid Blyton's
Orphans join a circus or leave
With the Gypsies!
Which should I do?'

I contact three of the kids.
Bobby and Tommy
Are both in Leeds
Caz is local and says
To meet up at Bank House.

We go straight there.
There she is – in her room
On the bed, in the foetal position
With no teeth – looking tiny
And it occured to me...

We really do go full circle.
Cradle to grave and round again
I knew that death was inevitable
But for all the hard work
In the last years -

And all her judgement
Of the teen years and all
The eye-rolling and sighing
Because of my behaviour
(She conformed – I didn't)

And all the times
That she was disappointed
By her daughters - and life -
And unhappy with being married...
She was a brilliant mum.

Or, as Germaine Greer says,

'The only good mother is a mother who died young, leaving a shining after-image against which all other mothering figures could be measured and found wanting'.

(The Whole Woman, 1999:249)